THE AGE OF BLISS–2

ABU BAKR

AS-SIDDIQ

RUHİ DEMİREL

NEW JERSEY • LONDON • FRANKFURT • CAIRO

TUGHRA
BOOKS

Copyright © 2015 by Tughra Books

18 17 16 15   1 2 3 4

Translated by Asiye Gülen
Edited by Clare Duman

Published by Tughra Books
345 Clifton Ave., Clifton,
NJ, 07011, USA
www.tughrabooks.com

Library of Congress Cataloging-in-Publication Data

Demirel, Ruhi.
[Hazreti Ebubekir. English]
Abu Bakr as-Siddiq / Ruhi Demirel ; translated by Asiye Gülen ; edited by Clare Duman.
pages cm. -- (The age of bliss ; 2)
ISBN 978-1-59784-371-3 (alk. paper)
1. Abu Bakr, Caliph, -634-Juvenile literature. 2. Caliphs--Biography--Juvenile literature. I. Gülen, Asiye. II. Duman, Clare. III. Title.
DS38.4.A28D4613 2015
953'.02092--dc23
[B] 2015013466

ISBN: 978-1-59784-371-3

Printed by
Imak Ofset, Istanbul - Turkey

TABLE OF CONTENTS

A Child Is Born

*I*t was the year 573 A.D. Two years had passed since the Year of the Elephant. The air in Mecca was scorching. Even the shade gave no relief from the heat. While some washed their faces and necks to cool off, others used fans.

A man came running into the bazaar shouting exuberantly, "Abu Quhafa, glad tidings! You have a lovely child!"

Abu Quhafa stood, shocked, for a moment, not knowing how to react. His first feeling was immense joy followed quickly by anxiety. Amid the hearty congratulations from those around him, Abu Quhafa said, "I hope he doesn't die like the others."

He hurried home and, taking the baby from the arms of his wife, Salma, he hugged the newborn with great love and their home was blessed with happiness.

A few days later, swaddling her baby, Salma left her house, filled with joy and anxiety. She was taking her baby to the Ka'ba. Stepping into the courtyard of the sacred building, without even glancing at the idols, she walked straight up to the Ka'ba itself and gently raised up her child, saying, "O Lord of the Ka'ba! All my children before this baby are with you now. It was not my fate to see them grow up. Please give this baby to me. Grant him a long life." Tears streaked her face and beautified her prayers as she pleaded to Allah with all her heart.

When she turned to leave she heard a voice whose words shook her to her core, "O servant of Allah, don't be anxious. Your request was accepted. Your child is going to live. He is going to be the closest Companion of the Messenger of Allah."

Salma was dumbstruck. She looked around in astonishment and, on seeing no one next to her, realized this was not a human voice. She prostrated in thankfulness then quickly returned home, not mentioning the strange incident to anyone.

From that day onwards, she devoted herself to bringing up her son with great care. Whenever Abu Quhafa and Salma looked at their child, whom they named "Atiq," they thanked Allah that he was alive.

Little Atiq, who would be known in the future as Abu Bakr, may Allah be pleased with him, was growing up. He could speak and express himself and his problems. He enjoyed playing games in the street with his friends and was loved by everyone. Even his neighbors admired him and talked about him with praise, praying that their children would be as morally upright as he was.

Idols

One day, Abu Quhafa hurried excitedly to his home. Drawing his child close to him, he said happily, "My dear son, let's visit the Ka'ba. Today they are setting out the big deities in the Ka'ba courtyard."

Without any objection, Atiq calmly prepared himself and set out with his father. On arrival at the Ka'ba, Abu Quhafa pointed out both the small and the big stones to Atiq saying, "Look, my son, these are our gods. They help us in all we do. We ought never be disrespectful to them. We kneel down in front of them and pray. You should know our deities too. Know them well! They are our biggest deities."

Little Atiq had lost interest in what his father was explaining. His gaze was fixed on a man dressing a stone. He couldn't understand why a man was dressing a stone that he had found himself and brought from the desert. Soon, another statue was brought outside. People were kneeling in front of it in supplication, requesting that their demands be fulfilled by the idol.

"My dear son, did you hear what I said?" asked Atiq's father. Atiq turned to look at the statues his father was describing. They were neither beautiful, nor peaceful but had terrifying expressions carved on their faces. Atiq refused to kneel down or show any respect to the stones, despite his father's insistence.

A while later, leaving Atiq at the Ka'ba, Abu Quhafa returned to his work. Atiq immediately approached the nearest idol saying, "I'm very hungry. Can you give me some food?" There was no sound from the idol so he requested, "Then, give me water." When the idol didn't respond, Atiq turned to another saying, "Give me clothes." He was unable to elicit a reaction from that idol either. To him, the stone and wood statues seemed inanimate, no different to any other pieces of rock or wood.

Thereupon, little Atiq took a stone from the ground. He came before a statue with flies buzzing all around it and said, "Now, I'm going to throw this stone at you. If you are really a god, then guard yourself!" He threw the stone fast and hard at the idol.

The people who witnessed this quickly sent word to Abu Quhafa who came running to the Ka'ba. On seeing what his son had done, he was shocked. He grabbed him by the arm and pulled him home, relaying everything to Salma when they arrived.

He worried, "I'm afraid this child is not going to worship our gods." Salma recalled the voice she heard in the Ka'ba when Atiq was just a baby. She caressed her son's hair, defending him to his father, "Do not interfere with him. Let him behave the way he wishes to. Tell him, the rest is up to him. Don't make him sad or unhappy by forcing him to do something he does not want to."

Shepherd

"*A*tiq, my son! Go and share this meat among the neighbors and, at the same time, send them my best wishes." Salma said, giving Atiq a tray of meat. Little Atiq took the tray and gazed lovingly at his mother with his deep-set eyes. Becoming aware of him, Salma nodded towards the door saying, "Don't mess around. Give the meat out quickly. You need to put the herd out to graze before it gets too hot outside."

Atiq hurried out and distributed the meat to the neighbors, one by one. The neighbors were filled with gratitude saying, "It was not spoken in vain! Those in difficulty are helped by Umm al-Khayr

(Mother of Goodness)." This was the nick-name given to Salma who was well-known for her works of charity. "We thank your mother for all the favors she has shown us."

On returning home with the empty tray, little Atiq was greeted by his father who was preparing to leave for Yemen for trade. He called to his son, "My dear son, take the herd from the stable, put them out to graze and give them water at the oasis. But be careful, don't let them stay out too long under the sun. Also, don't move them around too much, or they will be tired."

It was Atiq's responsibility now to take the herd out of Mecca every day for grazing. At noon he would rest in whatever small shady spot he could find. This ascetic lifestyle continued for years. Atiq grew into a young man and people started to call him "Abu Bakr."

The Caravan

The Meccans' made their living primarily through trade. They travelled in caravans to nearby cities, trading many different goods. Abu Bakr began to join these caravans buying many goods and selling them quickly. His skill and honesty gained him a good reputation and people began to trust him.

It was a summer's day. The scorching sun blazed down from its zenith onto the long caravan slowly making its way from Mecca. Making a break from their journey, shades were put up as everyone desperately sought relief from the sun.

"Hurry, let's take out our idols and pray." said one of the traders. Observing from a quiet corner, sat a thoughtful man. He was thin, of average height, with a close-cropped hair and a pale face.

The other traders didn't notice Abu Bakr's strange look as they hurried to take out the idols they had prepared themselves from halva. Prostrating in front of their home-made gods, they pleaded for everything imaginable; wealth, profits, health and even for money to pour from the sky.

"Enough worship," called the eldest from among them. "It's time to eat and drink." And so, it was time for the most entertaining part. The miniature idols, melting in the midday heat, that moments before had been prostrated in front of and supplicated, were shared between the traders and eaten. The men laughed and joked with each other as they chewed the sweet, sticky halva.

"My wife cooked this idol yesterday evening. How is it? Did you like it?" called out one man. "How could you say 'like'? It is delicious! But next time tell your wife to use more sugar," replied an older man, laughing.

One of the traders called out to Abu Bakr, wine dripping from his mouth onto his chest as he spoke. "O son of Abu Quhafa! You didn't pray to our gods, you didn't eat any halva. At least take a sip of our wine."

Looking at the man's face, Abu Bakr felt disgusted. As he prepared to answer, another man called out, "Hey you! Don't you know Abu Bakr? He doesn't pray to our gods and he doesn't drink our wine. No one has ever seen him drinking."

Wiping his mouth on his sleeve, another man interrupted, "Well done to him! He is one of just a few men in Mecca who has never tasted wine. His best friend, Muhammad, never drinks either."

Abu Bakr decided to keep quiet. He was often witness to such events and watched this strange behavior with great sorrow. He would never act in this way, nor would he ever keep idols in his home.

With the eating and drinking finally over, the caravan continued its journey until nightfall. That very night, Abu Bakr had a strange dream that the moon flew down from the sky, into his arms. As he pressed it to his chest he awoke, filled with curiosity and excitement.

Understanding this was no ordinary dream, Abu Bakr asked those around him to explain it, but to no avail. At last, they remembered a wise man, who might be able to help him, living in Yemen.

As soon as Abu Bakr arrived in Yemen, he searched out the wise man and related his dream, hoping for an explanation.

"Where are you from?" asked the wise man.

"I'm from Mecca."

"What are you doing?"

"I'm a merchant."

The wise man smiled. Looking meaningfully at the young man in front of him he said, "Your dream brings joyful news." Abu Bakr listened impatiently as he continued, "The moon in your dream is the last Prophet that God will send. He will soon be revealed to us. You are going to be his closest friend and his helper."

The wise man's words made a strong impression on Abu Bakr. Everyone was already talking about the imminent arrival of a Prophet and these glad tidings could also be found in the Torah and the Gospel.

Abu Bakr had never dreamed that he would be the closest Companion of the coming Prophet. The wise man continued, "In return for my glad tidings about the blessed Prophet, I want to request something from you. If I am still alive when his identity is revealed, please send me news. I want to meet him. If I have already died, send him my best wishes and be a witness that I have already accepted whatever he will bring."

Abu Bakr was consumed in deep thought throughout the entire homeward journey to Mecca. Upon his return, he started to carefully follow what was happening around him in the city.

Submission without Hesitation

$\mathcal{A}$bu Bakr sat at home, his eyes transfixed on a spot on the wall, his mind lost in thought. He couldn't stop thinking about the news people were telling each other. All the Jewish and Christian scholars were talking about the imminent arrival of a new Prophet. A wise man himself, Abu Bakr had also read this good news in the Torah and the Gospel.

He straightened up suddenly and headed for the door. He would visit his friend, Muhammad, peace and blessings be upon him, who was known as "al-Amin" (the Trustworthy) and discuss the problem with him. He walked along, mulling over the news and talk he had heard so far, when he saw that very friend approaching.

Joy washed over his face as he confronted the one with whom he shared all his problems, the one whom he loved as a brother and the one whom he always found trustworthy.

Exchanging looks of fraternal love, Prophet Muhammad, peace and blessings be upon him, asked, "Where are you going, Abu Bakr?"

"O Muhammad! I was coming to you. I was going to tell you something. But where were you going?"

From the look on his face, Abu Bakr understood that his friend was preparing to tell him something important. And so, it happened as he expected. The most truthful among all men opened his mouth and slowly articulated his powerful message. "I am the servant and Messenger of Allah. Allah has sent me with his covenant to humankind. I invite you to worship the Unique One! I swear to Allah that my claim is true."

Abu Bakr listened with bated breath. The words rang beautifully in his ears. The good news that everyone had spoken of was real. The final Prophet had come at last.

"O Abu Bakr!" the Messenger of Allah said, "I invite you to Allah! I call you to worship only Him, and not to hold any other deity beside Him. And in the path of making people believe in Him, I call you to help me."

"What evidence do you have to prove the truth of your claim?"

"The wise old man you came across in Yemen," and the newly announced Prophet related word for word what he had said to Abu Bakr.

Upon hearing this, Abu Bakr could not deny it. He believed his friend wholeheartedly.

Abu Bakr looked at the noble Prophet's illuminated face affectionately. It was as if he had been waiting for this moment for years. With his heart beating wildly, he leaned forward and took his friend's hand. His heart, blooming with the deepest love, Abu Bakr said the most beautiful of all words, "I bear witness that there is no deity but Allah, and I bear witness that Muhammad is His Messenger." With his heart as light as a bird, Abu Bakr experienced the pure joy of being one of the first Muslims.

Invitation to Allah

The number of the Muslims had reached thirty-eight. They were gathered in the house of Arqam, looking at the noble Prophet, their hearts filled with happiness. They had finally been guided to the straight path and, with him to lead them, vowed not to stray from this way.

However, outside of their sanctuary, hundreds of people were still living a life full of immorality and needed to be enlightened about the beauty of Islam, regardless of the risks that lay in spreading this message.

Abu Bakr looked at the noble Prophet's smiling face and said, "O Muhammad! Let's go out together and invite people to Islam so they will share this happiness too."

The Messenger of Allah looked at Abu Bakr with affection and replied, "We are not many people now." Upon hearing this, Abu Bakr insisted until Prophet Muhammad, peace and blessings be upon him, could no longer resist his pleas and they set out for the Ka'ba together.

On arrival, they wandered around for a while, then each sat near his own relatives and started to explain the divine message. Later, Abu Bakr stood and gave a speech calling the polytheists to the path of Allah with the noble Prophet watching from a corner.

The people at the Ka'ba looked at Abu Bakr with hatred and hostility, muttering, "Look at that man. He has forgotten that he came to Mecca for these idols. If we give up worshipping our gods, nearby tribes will do the same. Then Mecca will no longer be an important trading center. We won't earn any money. We will run out of food, and starve!"

The murmurs grew louder, with people growing angry and calling, "So what are we waiting for? Let's silence the one speaking down to us!"

With hearts full of anger, the polytheists attacked the Muslims, punching and kicking them, intending to kill them. There was one man in particular who went wild with anger; Utba thought his punches were not enough and he started to kick Abu Bakr with his iron shoes. Abu Bakr's face swelled but this was not enough for Utba; he climbed on top of Abu Bakr who was lying face-down in the dirt and continued to attack until Abu Bakr fell unconscious. Onlookers began to wail in terror, "Abu Bakr must be dead!"

"Look! The people of the tribe of Taym are coming!"

A group of men from the same tribe as Abu Bakr ran into the brawl and broke up the angry mob. Despite not being Muslim, these men shared the same blood as Abu Bakr and would save him at any cost. Upon finding Abu Bakr, one of them said, "He is unconscious. We must carry him away carefully without disturbing him. Hurry! Bring a sheet!"

From his position lying face-down on the ground, Abu Bakr was carefully moved onto the piece of cloth and taken home where everyone expected he would die of his injuries. The men from the tribe of Taym returned to the Ka'ba and angrily threatened the perpetrators, particularly Utba.

"If Abu Bakr dies, we swear that we will also kill Utba!"

The polytheists had beaten Abu Bakr to within an inch of his life. His relatives stood around him waiting, without any hope that he would recover. His state was so wretched, he couldn't even speak.

After a long while, he moved his lips and, after looking slowly at the people around him, asked, "How is the Messenger of Allah?" Despite this improvement in his condition, the people around him became angry, "This happened to you because of him, yet you are still thinking of him and not of yourself and your own injuries. Shame on you! You put yourself in danger for no reason. Those men would have killed you if we had not arrived in time. However, it seems you haven't learned anything from your beating."

Abu Bakr ignored them and continued to ask about the state of the blessed Prophet who had been kicked repeatedly during the fight. "Is the Messenger of Allah alive? Has anything happened to him?" His concern for Prophet Muhammad, peace and blessings be upon him, was a thousand times greater than his concern for himself. He wished, "Let thousands of Abu Bakr's be sacrificed for him." Truly, he understood what it meant to be Muslim.

The Truthful One

Fully recovered from the injuries he had sustained during the fight at the Ka'ba, Abu Bakr was wandering around the streets of Mecca when a group of men hurried towards him in a state of excitement. When they came closer, one of them called to him, "O Abu Bakr, did you hear the news? Your companion, Muhammad, claims he made a forty-day journey in just one night. He supposedly went from the Ka'ba to Al-Aqsa mosque in Jerusalem, and then up into the sky from there."

Abu Bakr's eyes widened with surprise, "Are those truly his words?" One of the men smiled and waited for Abu Bakr to protest, "This is impossible!" The man stepped forward, saying hopefully, "Of course, this is not a believable thing to say."

Abu Bakr stared at the men, then said with devotion, "I don't think the same way as you. If Muhammad has said this, it is certainly true. Have you ever witnessed him tell a lie, even jokingly?"

The polytheists were taken aback and, for a moment, didn't know how to reply. One of them pulled himself together, saying, "What? So do you believe all of this?"

Abu Bakr shrugged, "Without a doubt, I do!"

This was not the answer the men had hoped to hear. They persisted, "How can it be? Going to Jerusalem in such a short time and traveling through the skies, then returning before morning. These are not possible things. Abu Bakr, you are a wise man, how can you believe this?"

"It's not just this, I also believe in the words that the angels bring down from the skies. The really incomprehensible thing is your position. On the one hand, you call him 'al-Amin,' the Trustworthy, yet on the other hand you don't believe his words" said Abu Bakr.

And so the polytheists turned away, not finding what they had hoped for in their conversation with Abu Bakr who had displayed an unexpected attitude.

Witnesses to this event related what they had seen to Prophet Muhammad, peace and blessings be upon him, who was so pleased with what he heard, he began to call Abu Bakr "as-Siddiq" (the Truthful) due to his unhesitating affirmation of the truth. From now on, Abu Bakr was always known by this name.

Bilal Is Free

The polytheists could not accept the increasing spread of Islam. They tried everything they could think of to prevent people from becoming Muslim. This included oppressing and torturing those Muslims who were poor or without family to protect them. They went as far as rolling them up in mats and burning them or leaving them to die of thirst and starvation.

Abu Bakr was protected by his tribe and the polytheists were no longer able to harm him. Taking advantage of this situation, Abu Bakr walked the streets of Mecca unashamedly, telling everyone he met about Allah.

One day, a man came running to Abu Bakr and whispered something in his ear. Abu Bakr sprang to his feet and started running like the wind. He ran until he came upon a large crowd, laughing under the scorching desert sun, thoroughly entertained by whatever it was they were witnessing.

Suddenly, the sound of the laughter was pierced by an awful cry, followed by someone shouting, "You will die in this way, Bilal, or else you will deny Muhammad and worship Lat and Uzza instead!" A wailing voice responded, "There is but one Allah! There is but one Allah!"

Curiously, Abu Bakr made his way to the front of the mob and stopped, frozen by the awful scene he encountered. Lying on the ground in front of him was an Abyssinian slave. A huge stone had been placed on top of him, so large he could not get up. The black slave was a new Muslim named Bilal.

Unable to bear the situation any longer, Abu Bakr confronted the slave's owner, Umayya, exploding with hatred, "What do you want from this poor slave? Aren't you afraid of Allah? When will this torture end?"

Umayya looked at Abu Bakr, his frown distorting his ugly features. He snapped back sarcastically, "You're the one that has put him in this situation. Why don't you save him?" This was an insinuating offer. Umayya had no further use for Bilal and he intended to sell him to Abu Bakr.

"OK! Let's do it like this then," retorted Abu Bakr. "I have a slave of your religion. He is also stronger than Bilal. I'll give him to you in exchange for Bilal."

Umayya was a cold-hearted man; a misanthropist to the core, he had what he wanted, but he was going to wring this deal for everything it was worth. Holding everyone present as a witness, he said, "But I have a condition. You are also going to give me his wife."

"OK. I accept your demand."

"I'm not finished. I also want their children."

"OK. I accept that too. Do you have any other conditions?"

"No. I accept our deal. Take Bilal, he's yours."

Happy with this result, Abu Bakr rushed forward and removed the stone from Bilal saying, "Stand up, Bilal. Now you are safe." Then, along with six other slaves that he saved from persecution, he granted Bilal his freedom.

Protection

Life was becoming increasingly difficult for the Muslims in Mecca. The oppression and persecution they received from the polytheists was increasing daily and had reached almost unbearable proportions.

Abu Bakr would often sit outside reciting the Qur'an loudly, moved to tears by the words. This habit elicited the attention of the women and young people in Mecca who would pass by, looking at him in astonishment. They started to talk about him among each other. "How strange! What is that man reading?"

"His voice is so moving."

"Look! Abu Bakr is crying!"

Abu Bakr didn't pay any attention to these people or their gossip. He barely noticed them and continued performing long prayers, reading and crying. The passersby began to take more notice of his soulful recitation of the verses, listening with admiration. They gathered closer and closer each day, pushing each other out of the way in order to catch a glimpse of Abu Bakr.

The polytheists were not happy with this situation. They took to warning Abu Bakr but he ignored their warnings and continued to read the Qur'an aloud, crying openly as he read.

Seeing that the situation was not improving, the polytheists sent a group to speak with him. The group confronted Abu Bakr face to face, threatening him.

"O son of Abu Quhafa! We cannot stand your weeping and crying anymore. If you continue to worship in front of everyone who walks by you, our women and our children, you will experience severe repercussions!"

Abu Bakr was upset by these threats and reported the situation to the noble Prophet, "O Messenger of Allah, these unbelievers are trying to prevent me from worshipping. How can I ignore their threats? Please give me permission to do something. I want to go a place where no one can interfere with my prayers."

The blessed Prophet instructed him to leave Mecca and go to Abyssinia where he would be able to worship freely without being threatened by unbelievers.

With a heavy heart, Abu Bakr set off on his journey, sad to leave both Mecca and his valued companion behind. After a while, he came upon a tribe whose leader, Ibn ad-Daghina, recognized him and enquired, "Where are you going, O Abu Bakr?"

Abu Bakr glanced sadly back at Mecca and spoke of his feelings, hoping that sharing them would lessen his grief at leaving the beloved Prophet and his city. "I can't bear the oppression we Muslims face in Mecca and so I have left. I'm going to a place where I can worship in peace."

Ibn ad-Daghina was not a Muslim; however, he loved Abu Bakr as a brother and said, "O Abu Bakr, one like you shouldn't leave his hometown. You are a hospitable person who helps his poor relatives.

Return to Mecca. Perform your prayers in your hometown. I will protect you."

So, the two men returned to the city together and, true to his word, Ibn ad-Daghina visited the most important men among the Quraysh (the most powerful tribe in Mecca) and informed them of his protection of Abu Bakr. "Abu Bakr is not a person to be thrown out of his hometown like a stray dog. How dare you dismiss such a good man from his own city? Don't forget this—from now on, Abu Bakr is under my protection, and no one can hurt him."

Ibn ad-Daghina commanded great respect from the people of Mecca and they were unable to object to him. However, they did put forward a condition. "It will be as you say! Abu Bakr can stay in Mecca. But, he should only worship at home. He can pray and read whatever he wants inside his house. Our women and children are too affected by him when he prays openly outside, reciting loudly and weeping."

Ibn ad-Daghina listened to them and said, "I will convey your words to him. But, you must be sure that Abu Bakr is under my protection from now on. Whoever wishes him harm, must contend with me first!"

Ibn ad-Daghina told Abu Bakr what the polytheists had said and from that day, Abu Bakr confined himself to the four walls of his house when performing worship.

Eventually, however, he couldn't resist praying outside so he built a small mosque in the courtyard of his house and continued to worship there. As usual, he read the Qur'an loudly and was moved to tears by the beauty of the words.

Passersby could clearly hear Abu Bakr from his mosque as he worshipped. On hearing his recitation, curious people gathered in the courtyard and were affected by his behavior. The unbelievers were unable to do anything as Abu Bakr was under the protection of Ibn ad-Daghina. According to this custom, no one could touch a person who was under the protection of someone more powerful.

Feeling powerless from this situation, the unbelievers at last found a solution to their problem. They sent a courier and invited Ibn ad-Daghina to Mecca. On his arrival, the polytheists angrily informed him of the situation. "We accepted your order and let Abu Bakr worship at home. But he has overstepped the mark and made a small mosque outside in his courtyard. There he openly prays and reads the Qur'an. Anyone walking by can hear him, and his recitation and prayers make an undesirable impression on our women and young people"

The men were visibly stressed, their hatred of Abu Bakr showing in their actions. With hearts hardened from years of worshipping stone idols, they laid out their intentions to Ibn ad-Daghina.

"Order him not to pray here. If he wants to worship inside his house, and only inside his house, he may do so. But, if he does not accept these terms, tell him you will remove your protection and backing. We respect you, and therefore we will not touch anyone under your protection. But, if he keeps on worshipping so openly, we will not allow it, regardless of the consequences."

Without saying anything, Ibn ad-Daghina left. He could see that the Meccans were very agitated this time and didn't want to confront them. Instead, he immediately went to Abu Bakr, telling him, "You know the conditions under which I hold you in my protection. You must either continue to act in accordance with them, or openly reject my patronage. I don't want to hear the Arabs saying that I break my word."

Despite the harshness of the words he heard, Abu Bakr was relieved. He had begun to tire of the burden of being under another man's protection and was not upset by the situation. He replied to Ibn ad-Daghina, "Here, you may have your patronage back! The patronage of Allah is enough for me."

On hearing Abu Bakr's words, Ibn ad-Daghina returned to the Quraysh leaders and told them, "Quraysh! The son of Abu Quhafa has relinquished my patronage. From now on, it doesn't matter to me; do what you want. I am not getting involved in your business."

Following his meeting with Ibn ad-Daghina, Abu Bakr decided to walk to the Ka'ba. While he was walking, one of the ignorant Quraysh polytheists appeared in front of him. Taking advantage of this opportunity to abuse him, the man threw some earth in Abu Bakr's face.

Abu Bakr was enraged by this action and turned to the onlookers complaining, "Do you see what this rogue is doing to me?" However, the men around him knew who he was and replied, disdainfully,

"You brought this situation upon yourself! If you were like everyone else, this wouldn't happen to you. Why did you oppose your own people?"

Abu Bakr was so upset by these words and actions. His immaculate heart couldn't comprehend the cruelty of the unbelievers. As he continued on his way to the Ka'ba, words poured from his lips, "O Lord, how much patience you have! O Lord, how much patience you have! O Lord, how much patience you have!"

Permission for Hijra

*A*bu Bakr and his daughters, Aisha and Asma, were disturbed by a rapid knocking at the door. Quickly opening the door, they were momentarily dazzled by light. This was not the light from the sun, it was the divine light emitting from Prophet Muhammad, peace and blessings be upon him. Unused to being visited by him at this time of the day, the three of them were filled with anxiety. The noble Prophet was a frequent visitor to the house in the early morning and evening, but never had he come during the daylight hours. Something important must have happened.

Worried, Abu Bakr asked, "O Messenger of Allah, you never come at this time. It must be something important that brings you here now?"

Looking around, the blessed Prophet noticed Aisha and Asma. "Please ask them to leave. I need to talk to you privately," he whispered to Abu Bakr.

"O Messenger of Allah, they are my daughters," Abu Bakr assured him, "my mother and my father would die for you. What is the matter?"

"The Almighty has given me permission to emigrate from Mecca."

Abu Bakr asked excitedly, "O Messenger of Allah! Will you allow me to come with you too?"

"I'm here to take you with me."

His eyes filling with tears, Abu Bakr couldn't hold himself. Crying for some time, he finally turned to the noble Prophet saying, "O Messenger of Allah, I have been preparing for this and have kept two camels for this purpose. You must take one of them."

The noble Prophet wouldn't accept the camel as a gift and offered to pay for it. Abu Bakr entreated, "O Messenger of Allah, you are worth the sacrifice of my entire family. You can pay for the camel if you wish, but let us go as soon as possible."

The preparations for the journey were completed. A guide was hired and a shepherd named Amir was instructed to bring them food and news of any developments in Mecca.

It was on a Thursday that Abu Bakr and Prophet Muhammad, peace and blessings be upon him, left the house by the back door and began their journey towards Mount Thawr.

As they travelled, Abu Bakr anxiously surveyed the land around them, worried that they had been noticed as they left. If so, he had to be very cautious and he often walked behind Allah's Messenger to protect him from any possible danger.

Noticing Abu Bakr's strange behavior, the noble Prophet asked, "O Abu Bakr, why you are sometimes in front of me and at other times behind me?"

Abu Bakr looked affectionately him saying, "O Messenger of Allah, sometimes I think we are being followed so I stay behind you. Sometimes I think they will ambush us from the front, so I walk in front to protect you."

Allah's Messenger smiled and with a voice full of love said, "So if we come across any danger, you are thinking you will confront it instead of me?"

Abu Bakr replied without hesitation, "Yes, I swear by Allah who sent you to bring justice, I won't let any harm come to you. I will confront anything or anyone that might hurt you."

Finally, the weary travelers arrived at a cave which seemed a good place to spend the night. Carefully climbing up to the cave entrance, Abu Bakr said, "O Messenger of Allah, permit me to go inside first and check the cave. It could be the burrow of a wild animal. Maybe there are snakes or centipede nests inside. Whatever might be inside, I do not want it to harm you."

Abu Bakr entered the cave, checking everything inside. He blocked some small holes with pieces torn off his shirt and, after assuring himself that the cave was safe and clean, he invited Prophet Muhammad, peace and blessings be upon him, inside. The noble Prophet stooped to enter through the small hole then settled comfortably next to Abu Bakr and they began talking.

Time passed without them noticing, they were so deep in conversation about Allah. It was late evening when they heard the sound of horses whinnying. Shortly after, they were disturbed by the voice of Umayya, the former owner of the slave Bilal and a great enemy of the Muslims.

"We searched every inch of Mecca, but could not find them. I swear by Hubel! I'll find them even if they are under the seven layers of the earth!"

Following which a scout was heard to say, "Considering their tracks, I think they must have headed up towards that cave over there."

Then came the excited voice of Abu Jahl, another great enemy of the Muslims. "Then why are we standing here? Let's go and get them!"

They could hear the men climbing the slope, shortly arriving in front of the cave.

Abu Bakr shook with fear. Holding his breath, he fixed his eyes on the entrance to the cave. "O Messenger of Allah," he whispered. "These men are going to catch us! If one of them just leans a little to look into the cave he will see us. I swear to Allah,

I'm not worrying about myself, I'm worrying about you!"

The blessed Prophet sat quietly and calmly without a trace of anxiety on his face. "Do not be afraid," he said peacefully to Abu Bakr. "Allah is with us."

Meanwhile, the men standing in front of the cave began to speak again. Umayya could be heard shouting angrily to the scouts.

"Didn't you see this spider's web covering the entrance to the cave? If they had entered from here, this web would have been torn. You brought us up here for nothing!"

The men grumbled angrily, then mounted their horses and rode away. Something as simple of a spider's web had protected the two holy travelers. This was truly a miracle from Allah. He had saved the believers, and they were able to continue safely on their journey.

Real Guide

Having rested in the cave for a few days, the blessed Prophet and Abu Bakr continued their journey on Monday morning. Traveling in the direction of Medina, they occasionally looked back longingly towards the homes they had left behind in Mecca.

After a while, Abu Bakr heard the noble Prophet say, "O Mecca, you are the most auspicious place Allah has created. You are the most beloved of Allah. Nowhere is better than you and there is no home more beloved than you. If my people had not forced me to leave you, I would not make my home anywhere else."

It was noontime and the sun beat down on the heads of the travelers, forcing them to look for shade. Looking around him, Abu Bakr spotted a group of rocks a little way ahead.

"There is a shady spot over there!" he said.

He rode ahead to investigate and saw that the shadow cast by the rocks gave only enough shade for one person. Clearing the brambles growing next to the rocks, Abu Bakr removed his garment and made a pillow from it which he placed on the ground.

He called to the beloved Prophet, "O Messenger of Allah, you can rest here a little. We can continue our journey later."

The noble Prophet was touched by his devotion. He lay down in the shady spot lovingly prepared by his Companion and rested.

Meanwhile, Abu Bakr went to take a look around. As he was checking whether they were being followed, he came across a young shepherd.

"Do you have a sheep you can milk?" he asked the shepherd.

"Yes," replied the shepherd.

"Then can you get some milk for us?"

Although the shepherd didn't know Abu Bakr, he agreed to give him milk. "Why not? Of course I can," he said. He milked one of his sheep, putting the milk into a container and passing it to Abu Bakr. Abu Bakr thanked the shepherd and took the milk to Prophet Muhammad, peace and blessings be upon him, who drank it when he awoke.

Abu Bakr asked, "O Messenger of Allah, shall we go now?" The noble Prophet stood up. The two companions loaded their goods back onto their camels and continued on their way.

Allah Protects His Messenger

The Meccan polytheists had promised a reward of one hundred camels to anyone who could capture the noble Prophet and Abu Bakr. Suraqa was an expert tracker and had received information about four men with two camels traveling along the coast road. Without losing any time, he set out on his horse towards the coastal path. Just as quickly, he found the people he was looking for. He spurred his horse onwards, stirring up the dust along the road as he lessened the distance between them.

Abu Bakr's heart started beating hard as he nervously watched the approaching horse. "O Messenger of Allah, there is a rider coming towards us!" he called to the blessed Prophet.

Deep in prayer and submission, the noble Prophet didn't hear Abu Bakr. With the rider swiftly approaching, Abu Bakr called out again. "O Messenger of Allah, he will catch us!"

Then the Allah's Messenger responded, "Do not be afraid. Allah is with us."

The rider drew closer and closer. There were only five to ten meters separating him from the noble Prophet. Abu Bakr recognized that the man wanted to harm his companion and he began to weep.

"Why are you crying?" asked the beloved Prophet.

"I swear to Allah, I'm not crying for myself. I'm crying for you," he replied chokingly.

Allah's Messenger turned to the rider and recognized him. It was Suraqa. His ambition to win the reward had driven his search and he had finally succeeded.

"I have caught you!" he shouted and rode up to them.

Just at that moment, the noble Prophet's voice was heard, saying, "O Allah, protect us from the evil this man intends towards us!"

Suddenly, Suraqa's horse sank into the sand. Abu Bakr was startled by what had happened. From where Suraqa had fallen to the ground he rose and tried to remount his horse to muster another attack. His horse fell and again sank into the sand. Smoke began to rise from the ground where Suraqa and his horse were stuck. Addressing the blessed Prophet, Suraqa implored. "I know that what is happening to me is because of you. If you'll rescue me I'll give up trying to catch you."

The noble Prophet prayed to Allah to save Suraqa and his horse and, miraculously, Suraqa was now able to free his horse from the sand and remount. He immediately set off towards Mecca, calling back to them, "My shepherds are not far from here. If you tell them how many sheep or camels you need, they will give them to you. You will have need of them in Medina."

The blessed Prophet smiled at him softly and prayed. Then he said, "We will not need them."

After Suraqa had ridden away, Prophet Muhammad, peace and blessings be upon him, and Abu Bakr continued on their path towards Medina.

Finally, the desolate desert roads ended and they began to come across people. As a frequent visitor to this area, Abu Bakr was well known and everyone who encountered him asked, "Abu Bakr, who is it that accompanies you?"

Abu Bakr responded to these questions without hesitation, "My guide!"

Abu Bakr was telling the truth. His companion was the noble Prophet who had shown him the right path and was his true guide.

Medina

On arrival in Medina, the blessed Prophet and Abu Bakr were welcomed with unprecedented enthusiasm. The Medinans invited the Muslims into their homes, thus earning the name *Ansar* (helpers). The emigrants were called *Muhajir* which derives from "migration."

A hospitable, gracious and elegant woman named Kharija invited Abu Bakr to her house and he began to stay at her house frequently. When the beloved Prophet declared the Muhajir and Ansar to be like brothers and sisters, Abu Bakr accepted Kharija as his sister, thus strengthening their friendship.

Meanwhile, the Muslims in Medina wanted to build a mosque as a place for the new community to congregate and worship together. Everyone was keen for the mosque to be built on their land, however, the most suitable land was agreed to be that belonging to two orphan children. When they were approached about this issue, the children quickly agreed to the plan, offering to donate the land without charge. They said simply, "O Messenger of Allah, we'll give you this land for free. Use it as you wish."

The noble Prophet, however, wanted to ensure the children received payment to the full value of the land. The Muslims met to discuss the issue of raising the money, when Abu Bakr offered, "O Messenger of Allah, I brought five thousand dirhams with me when we left Mecca. Please allow me to pay for this land."

The blessed Prophet agreed, and after paying for the land, Abu Bakr began the construction of the mosque. Abu Bakr and Muhammad, peace and blessings be upon him, worked together on the construction, both mixing and carrying the mud mortar. Finally, the Muslims of Medina had their mosque.

The Promise
of Paradise

One day, Abu Bakr went to visit the noble Prophet. He was sitting at home and Abu Bakr stood at the garden gate, waiting for permission to enter. The blessed Prophet enquired of another Companion who was waiting to visit. The Companion, pointing towards Abu Bakr with his finger, said, "It is Abu Bakr requesting for permission to come to see you."

On hearing this, the Messenger of Allah said, "Please tell him to come in, and give him the good news that he has a place in Paradise."

Smiling, the Companion approached Abu Bakr, saying, "O Abu Bakr, the Messenger of Allah announces that you have secured a place in Paradise!"

Words cannot describe the feeling of joy that bloomed in Abu Bakr's heart on hearing this news. He felt he was the luckiest man in the world. Praising and thanking Allah in his heart, he walked in and sat at the side of the noble Prophet.

Race for Favor

The news that the mighty Byzantine Empire was preparing an army to attack Arabia was spreading quickly throughout the peninsula. To prepare an army for the forthcoming battles, the blessed Prophet called his Companions for help.

Umar, one of the closest Companions of the noble Prophet, calculated all his property and went to see Allah's Messenger.

Allah's Messenger asked him, "Umar, what did you bring with you?"

"O Messenger of Allah, I brought half of everything I own."

Upon this the beloved Prophet asked, "What you have left your children?"

Umar, may Allah be pleased with him, answered, "I've left them the other half."

The noble Prophet was very pleased with this reply.

Soon after, Abu Bakr arrived. The Companions of the blessed Prophet always competed to outdo each other in faith and good deeds to earn both the pleasure of Allah and His Prophet. Umar was sure that this time he would have surpassed Abu Bakr's goodness in the eyes of the noble Prophet.

The Messenger of Allah asked, "Abu Bakr, what have you brought for the army?"

"Everything I have, I donated for Allah, O Messenger," he said.

The beloved Prophet asked, "Well, what did you leave your family?"

Abu Bakr answered, "I left them the love and good pleasure of Allah and His Messenger,"

Umar and all the other Companions who were present realized that it was impossible to outdo Abu Bakr when it came to exemplifying the true faith. That was a race that no one could win.

Hunger

One evening, Abu Bakr was suffering from hunger. Finding nothing to eat at home, he thought for a while about what he could do. He left his house and headed through the empty streets towards the mosque. On his way he met Umar. Surprised to see each other, Abu Bakr enquired, "O Umar, what brings you out so late?"

"Hunger... and why are you here?"

"I'm here for the same reason."

As the two friends looked for somewhere to rest, the noble Prophet arrived. He too was hungry and had come out in search of food. The blessed

Prophet said, "Get up! Let's visit Abu al-Haytham.
I'm sure he will offer us something to eat."

They walked to Abu al-Haytham's house but
found it silent when they arrived. Everyone was getting ready to sleep. Abu al-Haytham's youngest son
heard them knocking at the door and a voice calling
out, "Abu al-Haytham!"

The child sat up in bed and called his father,
"Father, Umar is at the door calling you."

Abu al-Haytham, may Allah be pleased with him,
called back, "Lay down son, you must have heard
wrong. Umar can't be at the door at this time of
night."

The child, however, couldn't sleep. He could still
hear the voices outside and heard another call, "Abu
al-Haytham!"

The child left his bed and went to rouse his
father. "Father, Abu Bakr is calling now. The best
friend of the Messenger of Allah is at the door!"

Abu al-Haytham couldn't believe that anyone
would be out at such a late time. "Go to sleep, son,"
he replied. "Why would Abu Bakr visit us at this
late hour. You must be mistaken."

Returning to his bed, the child still couldn't sleep and lay listening to the conversation going on outside. As he listened, he heard a third voice which filled his heart with joy. "Abu al-Haytham!"

Excited, the child jumped out of bed and ran to the door, shouting joyfully, "Father, get up! Allah's Messenger has come to our house!" He opened the door and saw the noble Prophet, Abu Bakr and Umar standing there. His eyes glowing with excitement, he looked at the three of them and said, "Welcome, O Messenger of Allah!"

At the same time, Abu al-Haytham came running and was just as excited to receive such guests. "What a great honor O Messenger of Allah! Please come inside," he said, welcoming them in.

Abu al-Haytham quickly went to the garden and gathered a variety of plums and dates from his orchard. He butchered one of his cattle and prepared a great feast with the meat for his guests. It was an enormous pleasure for him to serve these esteemed visitors. Their suffering was eased with the food which had been prepared for them with such sincerity and devotion.

Forbidden Bite

nother evening, Abu Bakr was again suffering from hunger pains. Just as he was about to leave home to look for food, a servant approached him with food in his hands. "O Abu Bakr, look, I brought you something. Here, eat," he said.

Abu Bakr started to eat and realized how hungry he really was. As he finished his last mouthful he noticed that his servant was looking at him strangely. He asked, "What's the matter? Why are you staring at me?"

"Whenever I bring you something to eat, you ask me where it came from," the servant replied. "But, this time you ate without asking."

"I was very hungry this evening," said Abu Bakr. "I suppose that is why I ate quickly without asking. Tell me then, where did you get this food?"

Folding his arms in front of him, the servant began, "As you are aware, before I became Muslim I used to prepare amulets and good luck charms. Once I prepared an amulet but the customer did not have the money to pay for it. Today, I was walking past their house and saw a celebration going on. I decided to collect their debt. They had the money and paid me."

Abu Bakr's face started turning red. Without realizing his mistake, the servant continued, "I bought this food with that money. How was it? Did you enjoy it?" he asked.

Abu Bakr was distraught and cried, "Oh, you have almost destroyed me!" Putting his fingers down his throat, he tried to vomit without success. After trying a few times he was unable to bring the food back up.

Watching Abu Bakr, the servant was very confused. Then, realizing what he was trying to do, he advised, "Drink water! Only if you drink large amounts of water can you make yourself vomit."

Abu Bakr quickly drank a large glass of water, and put his finger down in his throat again. This time he was successful in emptying his stomach. Sighing with relief he began to wash his hands and face.

The servant asked, "By the grace of Allah! All this was to bring back up what you just ate? What was so harmful about this food?"

"Even if it caused me to lose my life I would force myself to get this food out of my body," replied Abu Bakr, continuing, "because one day I heard the Messenger of Allah say, 'Whoever eats forbidden food, only hellfire will cleanse his body.'"

The servant stood, waiting for Abu Bakr's wrath, but Abu Bakr wasn't angry. He knew the servant gave him the food in good faith. He simply advised him to take more care in the future.

Visiting a Patient

One day, the noble Prophet was sat talking with his Companions. Casting his eyes around him, he asked, "Who among you fasted today?"

The Companions looked at each other. When no one replied immediately, they began to think that no one had fasted. Then, Abu Bakr spoke up, "I fasted today, O Messenger of Allah."

Smiling at this answer, the blessed Prophet asked another question, "Well, who visited a patient today?"

Again, it was Abu Bakr who answered positively, "I visited a patient today, O Messenger of Allah!"

The blessed Prophet asked a third question, "Who has attended a funeral today?"

"I have, O Messenger of Allah," Abu Bakr answered. Each time Abu Bakr answered his questions, the noble Prophet's face lit up with happiness.

"Well, did one of you give alms to the poor people, to help feed them?" the blessed Prophet enquired.

Again, it was Abu Bakr who responded, "I helped take care of a poor man today."

Looking lovingly at his friend, the beloved Prophet said, "Whoever does all of these good deeds in one day will have a place in Paradise!"

Discussion

One day, Abu Bakr and Umar argued causing Umar to become very angry. He turned his back on Abu Bakr and returned home. Running after him, Abu Bakr wanted to apologize, but Umar slammed the door in his face. Concerned, Abu Bakr ran to consult the noble Prophet about what to do.

When he saw Abu Bakr, the beloved Prophet immediately understood something was wrong and he looked at him questioningly.

Abu Bakr related what had happened, "O Messenger of Allah, Umar and I argued about something, and I think I hurt his feelings deeply. I ran after him, but he did not accept my apologies."

"May Allah forgive you, Abu Bakr," replied the blessed Prophet.

A short while later, Umar appeared at the noble Prophet's house. Entering quickly he expressed his regret at what had passed. He was worried that he had deeply insulted Abu Bakr.

Abu Bakr shook as he saw the noble Prophet frown at Umar. He felt responsible and said, "O Messenger of Allah, I swear I am guilty. It was my fault. I made Umar angry."

But the noble Prophet said to Umar, "Don't you offend my friend! Don't you offend my friend! When I first called people to believe in Allah, everyone said I was lying and refused me. Abu Bakr was the only person who didn't hesitate to join me!"

Every Soul
Tastes Death

*P*rophet Muhammad, peace and blessings be upon him, was addressing the Muslims in the mosque when Abu Bakr heard him say, "O my people! I swear to Allah, I was at the Pool of Kawthar for a few moments. Allah offered to give one of his servants the world, but the servant decided to go to the world beyond this one instead."

Upon hearing these words, Abu Bakr began crying, "I would sacrifice my father and mother for you, Messenger of Allah! We would sacrifice everything for you." he said.

The people were confused at Abu Bakr's words. Why was he saying such things? Then, thinking about what the noble Prophet had just explained they began to realize the meaning of his words. The servant at the Pool of Kawthar was him. He preferred to go to the world beyond this one, rather than accept this world.

Abu Bakr had immediately understood what the beloved Prophet was saying; that he had completed his mission in this world and would soon be going forth to the next.

It was indeed so. A few days later, the noble Prophet closed his eyes for the last time. His followers around his death bed were in a state of shock. It had never occurred to them that the blessed Prophet could die.

The Companions felt bereaved and stood around weeping. Unsheathing his sword, Umar cried out, "The Messenger of Allah did not die! He just fainted. Whoever says he is dead, I'll cut off his head with this sword!"

Through his tears, Abu Bakr looked at his beloved friend's face for the last time. "O Messenger of Allah!" he moaned in sadness. "You were so beautiful when you were among the living and you are also beautiful now that you are among the dead.

I swear by Allah Almighty you will not see a second death!"

Still in shock and unable to comprehend what had happened, Umar shouted out, "I'll break the neck of whoever says the blessed Prophet is dead. He's not dead!"

Abu Bakr interjected, "Be quiet, O Umar! Sit down! He is dead."

But Umar was in a state of denial. Looking at Abu Bakr with eyes full of tears, he said in an anguished voice, "Abu Bakr, do you truly mean this? You also?"

Abu Bakr did not answer. He turned towards the people around them and said, "O my people! Whoever believes in Muhammad should know he has died. Whoever believes in Allah should know that Allah is immortal! "

At this, Umar fell silent. Abu Bakr continued to talk.

"Don't you know that Almighty Allah made it known in the Qur'an that the noble Prophet will die like other people? Allah said to the blessed Prophet,

"You too will die; the polytheists awaiting your death will also die!"

It was as if the Companions were hearing this verse for the first time. Abu Bakr continued relating the verses, "Muhammad was a Prophet. There were many other Prophets before him. If he dies or is killed, will you turn back? Whoever would turn back, he should know that he cannot hurt Allah. Allah will reward those who are thankful."

Putting down his sword, Umar sank to his knees. "Every soul surely tastes death," he said mournfully.

Salary

ollowing the noble Prophet's death, Abu
Bakr was made Caliph of the Muslim state.
In the early days of his caliphate, Abu Bakr
was walking outside when he met Umar. After greet-
ing each other, Umar asked, "Where are you going,
O Chief of Believers?"

Abu Bakr replied, "To the bazaar."

"What will you do there?" asked Umar.

"Well, I will buy and sell goods. If I don't earn
any money, how can I care for my wife and child?"
he responded.

This reply caught Umar by surprised. How could
the Caliph have financial problems taking care of his

family? He sprang into action and went with Abu Bakr to visit Abu Ubayda, may Allah be pleased with them.

Explaining the situation to Abu Ubayda, Umar said, "O Abu Ubayda, Abu Bakr should only have to concern himself with the affairs of the caliphate. He shouldn't have to worry about providing for his family on top of running a government. We must give him a salary for running his household so that he can focus on more important work."

Abu Ubayda agreed. However, Abu Bakr interjected, "Allah gives you the best of intentions, but it is not lawful for me to accept a salary!"

Umar and Abu Ubayda would not be dissuaded, telling him that it was necessary. In the end, Abu Bakr was forced to accept, despite being unhappy with the situation. He would only agree to take a very low salary which was just enough to feed his family.

Humility

The Caliph, Abu Bakr, was out for a walk one day when he overheard a conversation.

"Abu Bakr used to help us with our work, but now he is the Caliph, he won't help us anymore for sure. Not now that he has so much power."

Turning to the woman who had spoken, Abu Bakr said, "Do not worry, my daughter. The son of Abu Quhafa will never change. As always, I will continue to help you with your work. I'll milk your sheep whenever you need it done."

Abu Bakr often helped this woman, but it was not enough for him. He exerted huge efforts to find people in need and helped them as best as he could.

One day, as he was returning home, he pondered how he could find those people who were most in need. As he walked, he spoke aloud to himself, "I wish I were wealthy enough to feed all the poor people everywhere."

He came upon a run-down old shanty house. Wondering if it was occupied, he knocked on the door. An old woman's voice came from inside, "Come in, the door is open!"

Opening the door gently, Abu Bakr peered inside. In the corner, an old woman was sitting. She said to him, "I'm blind and cannot see you. What do you want?"

Upset by her condition, Abu Bakr said, "I want to help you." It was clear to him that this woman had no one looking after her. "I'll come every morning and care for you," he said. And from that day onwards, that is what he did.

Army

efore his death, Prophet Muhammad, peace and blessings be upon him, had prepared an army, assigning the young Usama, may Allah be pleased with him, as the commander. The sudden death of the blessed Prophet prevented Usama from marching out with the army, and he kept them waiting for a while.

On being appointed Caliph, Abu Bakr ordered the army into action. However, there was a conflict in Umar's mind. While needed to fight abroad, the army might also be needed in Medina which was vulnerable to attack following the beloved Prophet's death.

Umar expressed his concerns to Abu Bakr, saying, "O Caliph, shouldn't the army remain in Medina?"

Abu Bakr was adamant, "By Allah, even if I knew that dogs or wolves would swoop down on us, I wouldn't make the army prepared by the Messenger of Allah wait any longer. Our noble Prophet himself established the army. Therefore, the army will continue marching on to where the Messenger of Allah ordered before he died!"

For some people, Usama's young age was a problem and they found it difficult to accept him as commander of the army. In their opinion, the army should have been commanded by someone older and more experienced. On hearing the murmurings about this, Umar went to Abu Bakr.

"O Chief of Believers," he said. "Some people are asking for an older commander."

Abu Bakr jumped up from his seat and grabbed hold of Umar's collar.

"Do you say so, O son of Khattab," he cried. "Was it me who appointed Usama as commander of the army? Our beloved Prophet himself assigned him to this position. How can you ask me to put someone else in his place?"

Umar himself agreed with Abu Bakr and so the army prepared for action under the leadership of Usama.

As the troops readied themselves to depart, Abu Bakr walked alongside them. Usama felt uncomfortable that the Caliph was walking while he and his comrades were mounted on horseback. Attempting to dismount to offer him his horse, Abu Bakr prevented him. Then, Usama gave the order for a horse to be brought for the Caliph. This was also refused by Abu Bakr.

"Please, let me dust my feet on the way of Allah," he said and continued to walk.

After walking for a while, Abu Bakr looked up at Usama and asked, "Can you allow Umar to stay with me in Medina?"

For a moment, Usama was dumbstruck. Abu Bakr was not only as old as his father, but he was the Caliph. He didn't need to request anything from Usama, he could merely order him, "I want Umar to stay with me." However, he asked permission from the commander of the army.

The onlooking soldiers were very impressed and their ambivalent feelings towards Usama evaporated. Usama granted permission for Umar to remain with Abu Bakr in Medina.

Following this incident, Abu Bakr made a speech to the army, outlining the rules of engagement for Muslims.

"Do not betray! Do not hurt anyone! Do not kill children, women or old people. Do not cut fruit trees and do not kill animals, only enough to suffice your nourishment needs but not for any other purposes. If you meet people of other religions or creeds, do not hurt them. May Allah be with you." With this, he bade farewell to the troops.

The Holy Qur'an

bu Bakr was well-loved by all the Muslims. No one had any complaints about him. He was skilled at administrating the state and, in suppressing some rebellions after the blessed Prophet's death, he provided peace.

In a short time, the army conquered new lands enabling the rapid spread of Islam. The battles, however, had seen the loss of many of those who knew the Holy Qur'an by heart.

This situation was worrying Umar who expressed his concern to Abu Bakr, "Many of the good men killed in battles were those who knew the Qur'an by heart. The number of such people is rapidly declining," he said.

Abu Bakr was also aware of this situation. "What can we do? Tell me your idea." he said.

"Let's gather the people and have them recite the verses in front of witnesses. Then we will write them and put them together as a book," suggested Umar.

"In the Name of Allah, I will not do something the Messenger of Allah himself did not do!" protested Abu Bakr.

Umar pressed Abu Bakr, outlying the merits of such a project and eventually managed to convince him. The project was started, the verses were written and, in a short time, the Qur'an came into being as a book.

Reuniting Day

Abu Bakr was in his sixty-third year, the same age the noble Prophet had been when he died. His two years as Caliph of the Muslims had not lessened the pain of being separated from his beloved Prophet. The absence caused by his friend's death made his days unbearable. He eagerly anticipated the day when they would be reunited.

The burden of managing the affairs of the state along with his great sadness caused him to become ill. He was nearing his last days.

One day, his condition suddenly deteriorated and he fell unconscious. He awoke to find his daughter,

Aisha, may Allah be pleased with her, crying at his bedside. He asked her, "Aisha, on which day did the Messenger of Allah die?"

In tears, Aisha replied, "It was a Monday."

"What day is it today?"

"Monday..."

Abu Bakr, hoped and prayed to die at the same age and on the same day as the noble Prophet.

"O Allah, take me to you today," he prayed fervently.

Then, turning to look at his daughter, he instructed, "Wash the clothes I'm wearing and wrap me in three cloths like the blessed Prophet. Then put me into the grave," he said.

Aisha spoke with difficulty: "But these are old clothes..."

"It doesn't matter," her father replied, "new clothes are for the living, the dead do not need them. They will rot in the grave."

He stared at the ceiling saying, "Thanks be to Allah. After serving as Caliph of the Muslims, I didn't receive a penny from them. I have only a slave, a camel for the water mill and this velvet fabric. These

are the belongings of the state. Give them all back."
This was his last will and testament which he com-
municated to his daughter.

Weeping, Aisha agreed with her father's request.

Shortly before his death, Abu Bakr called together
the elders from among the Companions. He asked
their opinion of Umar. Everyone responded positively about him and Abu Bakr declared. "I'm
appointing Umar, the son of Khattab, as your new
Caliph in my place. Listen to him and obey him. "

Without a moment's hesitation, everyone accepted the decree.

Abu Bakr departed the world to meet with his
Prophet and Allah. As his legacy, he left a camel and
a maid.

His mortal body was washed and prepared for
the grave by his wife. Umar, as the new Caliph, led
the funeral prayer and the best among Muslims was
buried in his final resting place beside his closest
friend and beloved Prophet. Shoulder to shoulder
in life, they were also side by side in death.

After a while, someone brought a pot of money
to Umar. "What's that?" he asked curiously.

"The remainder of Abu Bakr's salary... His request was to bring the money to you."

Umar emptied the pot. Seeing the small amount of money it contained he wept, "O Abu Bakr, may Allah have mercy on you! You have left us a very difficult example to follow."

From his childhood, throughout his youth and up until old age, Abu Bakr lived his sixty-three years with only goodness, grace and kindness. Allah and His Messenger were enough for him and they were pleased with him.

After Prophet Muhammad, peace and blessings be upon him, he was the most honorable among humans.

The words the noble Prophet used to describe him will not be forgotten until the Day of Judgment, "There is no one that we won't reward for their goodness. Except for Abu Bakr! He did so many good things that only Allah can reward him on the Day of Resurrection!"